# If Only Dad Could See Us!

Sheila M. Blackburn

The fifth book in Set A of
Sam's Football Stories

## Dedication
For My Mum.
With thanks to Tom for all the support
and understanding.

### Ackowledgements
With thanks to *The Boots Company* and *Delmar Press in Nantwich*,
for their support of this project.

**Published by Brilliant Publications**
1 Church View
Sparrow Hall Farm
Edlesborough
Dunstable
Beds LU6 2ES

Telephone: 01525 229720
Fax: 01525 229725
e-mail: sales@brilliantpublications.co.uk
website: www.brilliantpublications.co.uk

Written by Sheila M. Blackburn
Illustrated by Tony O'Donnell of Graham Cameron Illustration

© Sheila M. Blackburn 2002

**ISBN 1 903853 192 Set A – 6 titles: Football Crazy, Team Talk, Will Monday Ever Come?, Training Night, If Only Dad Could See Us! and A Place on the Team.**
ISBN 1 903853 036 Set B – 6 titles: The First Match, Trouble for Foz, What about the Girls?, What's Worrying Eddie?, Nowhere to Train and Are We the Champions?

Printed in England by Ashford Colour Press Ltd
First published in 2002
10 9 8 7 6 5 4 3 2 1

The right of Sheila Blackburn to be identified as the author of this work have been asserted by her in accordance with the Copyright, Designs and Patents Act 1988.

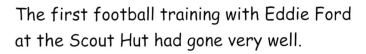

The first football training with Eddie Ford
at the Scout Hut had gone very well.

Sam was tired, happy and muddy
when he got back home.

"You need a bath," said Mum.

"I wish Dad had been there to see us," said Sam.

"You know he had to work, Sam," said Mum.

Mum had a lot of questions to ask.
"How was Eddie?
Was he any good?"

"He was brill," answered Sam.
"He was ace in goal."

"What about as a ref?" asked Mum.

"He was very fair," said Sam.

"David was mad – but he always is –
just because he didn't win."

"What did Eddie make of that?" asked Mum.

"Not much," said Sam.

"I wonder how you would feel if you lost?"

"I don't know," said Sam.

"It's important to learn how to lose," said Mum.

"Yes – I guess so," said Sam.

Sam dived onto his bed.
"What did it say in Eddie's letter, Mum?"

Mum opened the letter and read it aloud.

The letter said there would be twelve sessions and that Eddie was trying to fix up some matches.

"Wow! Great!" said Sam.
He was really excited.

The next Saturday afternoon, Sam was in the garden.

Eddie came to call.
He was on his old bike.
Sam heard it clanking up the street.

"Hello, Sam!"

"Hi, Eddie!"

Eddie was in his tracksuit.

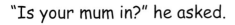

"Is your mum in?" he asked.

"She's in the kitchen. I'll show you."

Eddie had some things to ask Sam's mum.
He wanted to know if everyone was happy with the training.

Mum said she had talked to some of the other mums.
Everyone was pleased.

"Was the letter OK?" asked Eddie.

"It was fine," said Mum. "Danny's mum asked if his grandad could come and watch."

"Yes, of course," said Eddie. "I know he'll be a big help, too."

"Would you like a mug of tea?" asked Mum.

After his tea, Eddie went out into the garden with Sam.

"I see you have a soft ball," said Eddie.

"Yes. I broke the shed window last week.
It was a real football.
Dad says that this one is better for the garden."

"Good idea," said Eddie. "My mum and dad got very cross with me when I was your age. I broke lots of windows!"

Sam looked at him and smiled.

"Shall we try this ball out?" asked Eddie.

"Yeah. Great!" said Sam.

Eddie stayed for a while.

They tried some heading skills.
Eddie showed Sam how to flick the ball from foot
to foot.

They had a really good time. Sam was thrilled.

The time passed very quickly.
Then Eddie had to go. He went off on his old bike.

"Bye, Sam. See you on Monday at seven.
Don't be late!"

"I won't! See you, Eddie," Sam waved.

Sam picked up the ball when Eddie had gone.

"I wish Dad had been here to see us," he said.

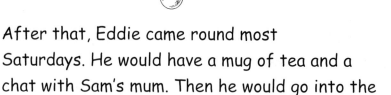

After that, Eddie came round most Saturdays. He would have a mug of tea and a chat with Sam's mum. Then he would go into the garden with Sam.

They always tried out some new moves and Eddie let Sam do some shots on goal. Sam loved those Saturday afternoons.

He wished Dad didn't have to work on Saturdays. He knew that Dad had to take the work when he could get it.

Sam really liked Eddie. He liked the way he went round on his old bike and waved to everyone. He liked him because he did the training for the lads. Most of all, he liked Eddie because he was so good at football.

"You should see the way Eddie dodges and tackles," Sam said to Dad one evening.

"Eddie can kick the ball really well and he hardly ever misses the goal."

"He sounds like a good coach," said Dad.

"He should play for United," said Sam.

Dad smiled.

"He's only playing against you lads, Sam," he said.

"Well ... I bet he's that good all the time," said Sam. "Anyway, Danny's grandad thinks Eddie's good, too."

"Oh, and if I can't play for United when I grow up,
I think I'd like to go to college, like Eddie.
You should see him, Dad. You really should."

Dad patted Sam on the head. "I'd like to, Sam,
but you know I have to work a lot.
Sometimes, it's very hard for me to go to work,
when I would rather be watching you.
Do you understand what I mean?"

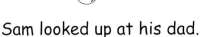

Sam looked up at his dad.

He thought about the broken shed window and how Dad had been so mad.

He thought about how they had worked together to clean up the shed and the game of football later on.

"Do you like football, Dad? I mean really like it?" Sam asked.

"Yes, I do, Sam," said Dad, "I was really mad about it when I was a lad. Just like you. I would love to come to see you. I really would."

"I know, Dad," said Sam.

On Saturday morning, Sam met Danny at the wasteland. The others hadn't come.

Danny hadn't got his football.
He was sitting on a log.
He kicked at the grass with the heel of his trainers.

"Hi, Danny!" said Sam.

Danny didn't look up.

Sam kicked the ball about.

"Come on, Danny. Are you playing?"

"No."

Sam went to sit by Danny.

He looked at his friend.
"What's up, Danny?"

Danny didn't say a thing.

Sam waited.

**If Only Dad Could See Us!**

At last, Danny looked up.
He was crying!
Danny never cried.
He ate a lot and talked a lot and always played football, but he never cried.

Something was very wrong.

Sam waited – Danny was his best friend.
He could wait all day.

At last, Danny said,
"It's my grandad. He's in hospital.
My mum says he isn't going to get better.
I went to see him and he said
he'd still like to come to see us play.
Mum says he can't come ... "

Danny hid his face in his coat.

Sam looked round the wasteland.

He didn't know what to say.
He wanted to do something.
Danny was such a good friend.

After a while, Sam said,
"I'm really sorry about your grandad."
Then he pulled his football stickers out of his pocket.
"Here, Danny," he said. "I want you to have all these
stickers. Let's go home."

Sam and Danny walked down the street without talking. Sam let Danny carry the football.

They went past Mrs Ford's shop.
Mrs Ford was at the window.
She watched them go past.
She knew all about Danny's grandad.

Back at home, Sam was very quiet.

"Do you want a drink?" asked Mum.

"No thanks," said Sam.

He went up to his room.

Mum waited a bit. Then she went up to see Sam.

He was lying on his bed.

"Are you OK, Sam? What's the matter?"
Mum sat on the bed and waited.

Sam asked, "Will Danny's grandad get better?"

"No, Sam. They really don't think so."

"Will he come out of the hospital?
Will he come and see us play again?"

Mum shook her head.

"It's not fair," said Sam.
He turned over and hid his face in his United bed cover.

Later on, Eddie came on his old bike.

Mum was in the kitchen.
She heard the bike as Eddie put it by the wall.
Mum put the kettle on.

"Hello. How are you all?"

"Fine," said Mum. "Sam is a bit sad."
She told Eddie what Sam had said.

"I know. My mum told me the news." said Eddie.
"Can I go up to see Sam?"

Eddie went up and sat on Sam's bed.
"Hello, Sam. My mum told me about Danny's
grandad," said Eddie.

Sam rolled over.
"I like Danny's grandad," he said.

"He's a really good man. He used to play a lot of
football," Eddie replied. "He even helped me to train
when I was a boy. Did you know that?"

"He was coming to see our first match.
Now he can't. It's not fair," muttered Sam.

After a while, Eddie said,
"Then let's make sure we win,
and we can use a few of the tricks that Danny's
grandad showed me."

Eddie waited.

Sam was thinking about it all.

At last, Eddie said, "Come on then, Sam.
Let's go and try them out."

Eddie made it good fun.
Sam had a great time.
However, he didn't forget about Danny and
his grandad.

On Monday at school, Danny was still sad.
Sam tried to cheer him up.
Miss Hill let them sit together in class.

It was a sunny day.
Mr Bond said they could all use the school field
again at break times.

Playing football on the field at playtime was really
good, but Danny didn't want to play.

He sat by himself. He said he was not going to
training.

"You have to be there, Danny!" said Sam.
"Eddie's fixed up the first match. He's going to
tell us about it. He's going to pick the teams tonight.
You want to be in the first team, don't you?"

"Maybe," said Danny. For the moment though, he
didn't want to play right now.

Sam felt very mixed up.

Miss Hill was on duty.

She saw Danny wasn't playing football.
She knew why.
"Best leave him," she said to Sam.

On the way home after school, Sam walked with
Danny. Sam talked about the match and the training.
He even told him what Eddie had said about Danny's
grandad.

Danny still said nothing.

At Danny's house, Sam said,
"Say you'll come tonight, Danny. Please!"

Danny looked hard at Sam.

"I'll call for you," said Sam.

Danny just looked.

"See you later, then," said Sam.

He turned to go. Then he turned back.
"Look, Danny. I know you feel sad, but ...
well ... I think ... your grandad likes football
such a lot, that it would make him really happy
if you got a place on the team – even if we lose
the first match."

Sam turned and ran all the way home.

After tea, Sam put his kit in his United bag.

"I'm off now, Mum. I'm calling for Danny, but I don't know if he'll come."

When he got to Danny's house, Danny's mum let him in. "Hello, Sam. I'm glad you're here."

Danny's bag was on the table.

"Is he coming?"

"Yes," said Danny's mum. "It's hard for him, but he is coming."

Danny came into the kitchen.
"Ready?" said Sam. "Let's go."

Eddie did a warm-up with the lads.

Then it was time to jog round the field.
They were a bit fitter now.
Most of them did three laps.

"Right, lads," said Eddie after the laps. "No time
for skills tonight. We'll get on with a game.

I need to watch you play so that I can pick a team."
"He only needs to pick eleven out of all of us," said
Sam.

"Plus subs," said Danny.

"Who will he miss out?" asked Sam.

"That's his job. He's the manager," said Danny.

"This is it then," said Sam. "Do your best for your
grandad, remember."

For the next part of the session, Sam played really hard. He was a forward and he liked that.

Foz was a better player.
He was centre forward.
Sam was glad to be on the same side as Foz and Danny.
Danny was playing well. Maybe he felt better.

He crossed the ball to Sam.
Sam struck it hard, but it just went over the bar.

Rob was in goal.
"Good shot, Sam. Nice try."

"I wish Dad was here to see this," Sam said to himself.

Sam's Football Stories

Sam was on the stronger side.
Tim was solid in defence.
He was doing some good tackling.

Ben was having a good game as goalie.
He didn't have as much to do as Rob.
Rob was very busy. Sam's team saw to that.

Especially Foz.

On a sudden break, Sam passed to Foz.
Foz hit it hard with his left foot. Rob dived to his
right and missed!

## "GOAL!"

yelled Foz.

He punched the air with his fist.

Eddie blew his whistle. The game was over and Sam's team had won 1-0.

They left the field.

"Boots!" yelled Eddie. He always did.
"Get changed, lads. Then come into the big room.
I'll tell you about the match and the team."

There was a lot of talking.
"Great goal, Foz."

"Good set-up, Sam."

Sam felt a hand on his back.
"Well done, Sam!"

He looked up.

"Dad! I thought you were working tonight."

"I finished early to see you play, Sam,
and I promised Danny's grandad that I'd give
him a full report. You did really well, too, Danny."

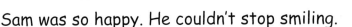

Sam was so happy. He couldn't stop smiling.

"I'm very proud of you, Sam," said Dad.

"Because you saw me set up that goal?"

"Yes – and because you're a good friend to Danny. His mum told me."

Sam nodded.
He didn't know what to say.

"Come on now," said Dad.
"Let's find out who Eddie's picked for the match on Sunday."

We hope that you enjoyed this book. To find out what happens next, look for the next book in the series.

## Set A

Football Crazy
Team Talk
Will Monday Ever Come?
Training Night
If Only Dad Could See Us!
A Place on the Team

## Set B

The First Match
Trouble for Foz
What about the Girls?
What's Worrying Eddie?
Nowhere to Train
Are We the Champions?